What You Don't Know about Turning 40....
A Funny Birthday Quiz

Bill Dodds

 Meadowbrook Press
Distributed by Simon & Schuster
New York

Library of Congress Cataloging-in-Publication Data

Dodds, Bill.
  What you don't know about turning 40 : a funny birthday quiz / by Bill Dodds.
     p. cm.
  ISBN 0-88166-509-6 (Meadowbrook)   ISBN 0-684-04000-X (Simon & Schuster)
  1. Middle age—Humor. 2. Middle aged persons—Humor. 3. Aging—Humor. I. Title.
  PN6231.M47D65 2006
  818'.5402—dc22

                    2005022663

Editorial Director: Christine Zuchora-Walske
Coordinating Editor: Megan McGinnis
Copyeditor: Angela Wiechmann
Editorial Assistant: Andrea Patch
Production Manager: Paul Woods
Graphic Design Manager: Tamara Peterson
Cover and Interior Illustrations: Steve Mark

Text © 2006 by Bill Dodds

Published by Meadowbrook Press, 6110 Blue Circle Drive, Suite 237, Minnetonka, Minnesota 55343

www.meadowbrookpress.com

BOOK TRADE DISTRIBUTION by Simon and Schuster, a division of Simon and Schuster, Inc., 1230 Avenue of the Americas, New York, New York 10020

18 17 16 15 14   20 19 18 17 16 15 14 13 12 11 10

Printed in the United States of America

Contents

Dedication

For Tom L. and Ruth—the Sarge and the Señorita

Acknowledgments

For their thoughtful reviews of this book's content,
Meadowbrook Press thanks the following people:

Polly Andersen, Bruce Brenckman, Beverlee Day, Laura Dyer, Val Escher, Dawn
Grapentin, Larry Holgerson, Kathy Kenney-Marshall, Trish Kuffner, Neal Levin,
Becky Long, Elaine Matthew, Judith McLaughlin, Eric Ode, Tami Peterson, Robert
and Diane Pottle, Ted Scheu, Maria Smith, and Christine Zuchora-Walske.

Chapter 1

Health & Beauty

Q: What medical term makes a 40-year-old shudder?

A: *Anything ending in -oscopy.*

Q: Is there anything good about reaching 40?

A: *Yes. Odds are, your acne has cleared up by now.*

Q: Do antiwrinkle creams aimed at 40-year-olds really do what they're designed to do?

A: *Yes. They're designed to make the manufacturers lots of money.*

Q: What do 40-year-olds hate?

A: *A mirror under fluorescent lighting.*

Q: What do 40-year-olds love?

A: *A mirror under dim lighting.*

Q: What's the most common back problem among 40-year-olds?

A: *Constantly telling younger people, "Back when I was your age…"*

Q: Why does the cosmetic industry focus on 40-year-old women?

A: *They're old enough to have tiny wrinkles and young enough to still see them.*

Q: Why do some call their 40th birthday a "wake-up call"?

A: *When they turn 40, they suddenly realize they have only three years to get in shape for their 25-year high-school class reunion.*

Q: Why should 40-year-olds refrain from plucking their gray hairs?

A: *Bald isn't beautiful.*

Q: Why does a 40-year-old need a strong heart?

A: *In a few years, she'll have to teach her teen to drive.*

Q: What's the first step in any exercise program designed for a 40-year-old?

A: *Get off the sofa.*

Q: Why are there so many tests during your physical when you turn 40?

A: *Your doctor wants to get a base line for comparison when things really turn bad.*

Q: What's a sure sign you're 40?

A: *You know the difference between "good" and "bad" cholesterol.*

Q: What do 40-year-olds call someone their age who runs marathons?

A: *Annoying.*

Q: What do 40-year-olds mean by "the F-word"?

A: Fiber.

Q: Why shouldn't you let a 40-year-old drink caffeine after 2:00 P.M.?

A: *He'll keep you up half the night, complaining that you let him drink caffeine after 2:00 P.M.*

Chapter 2

Work & Finances

Q: What's the easiest way for a 40-year-old to make her younger coworkers jealous?

A: *Telling them what she paid for her house ten years ago.*

Q: What's a 40-year-old's favorite fantasy?

A: *Calling the boss after winning the lotto.*

Q: What does a 40-year-old often think during the commute to work?

A: *Ferris Bueller had the right idea.*

Q: What's the difference between a 22-year-old college graduate and a 40-year-old worker?

A: *One dreams of how cool it will be to get a job; the other dreams of how cool it will be to not need a job anymore.*

Q: What are most 40-year-olds counting on for their retirement income?

A: *They're praying their junk from grade school will turn out to be valuable collectibles.*

Q: How does a 40-year-old describe her monthly income, more or less?

A: *More than she ever thought she'd make, but less than she's spending.*

Q: What's a sure sign you're 40?

A: *Your credit card limit is more than your first salary.*

Q: What's the hardest part about driving after you turn 40?

A: *Paying for gas at today's prices.*

Q: Why do 40-year-olds make good middle managers?

A: *They're used to their parents and their children being unhappy with them at the same time.*

31

Q: What's the difference between you as a teenager and you as a 40-year-old?

A: *Back then you cared about your 501 jeans, and now you care about your 401(k).*

Chapter 3

Recreation

Q: What's a 40-year-old's favorite celebrity news segment?

A: *"Where Are They Now?"*

THEN   NOW

Q: What's more pathetic than a 40-year-old trying to use the latest slang?

A: *A 40-year-old trying to do the latest dance.*

Q: What's a sure sign you've reached middle age?

A: *You can name more celebrities over 50 than under 30.*

Q: What does a 40-year-old call a night on the town?

A: *Exhausting.*

Q: What does a 40-year-old call music from ten to fifteen years ago?

A: *New.*

Q: Why do 40-year-olds talk about going back to school?

A: *It's been so long since they were in school, they've forgotten how bad it really was.*

Q: Why are 40-year-olds slow to buy the latest high-tech item?

A: *It comes with yet another remote they can't figure out.*

Q: What's a sure sign that a 40-year-old has admitted defeat?

A: *She doesn't hide the fact that she listens to the oldies station.*

Q: Why do 40-year-olds love their pets?

A: *Animals have no concept of age.*

Q: How do you know that a remote belongs to a 40-year-old?

A: *MTV isn't programmed in it. The Weather Channel is.*

Q: What do two 40-year-olds do on a wild night out?

A: *Split a dessert.*

Q: What's a sure sign you're 40?

A: *You double check that the waitress is really giving you decaf.*

Chapter 4

Aging

Q: Doesn't wisdom always come with age?

A: *No, but wrinkles do.*

Q: How does a 40-year-old begin a story about something that happened a decade earlier?

A: *"A few years ago…"*

Q: What's the difference between a 16-year-old and a 40-year-old?

A: *One throws her clothes on her bedroom floor, and the other hangs them on her exercise equipment.*

Q: When asked their age, why do 40-year-olds always hesitate and consider lying?

A: *They don't. It really takes them a moment or two to remember how old they are.*

Q: Why do 40-year-olds act a little dizzy?

A: *They've been around the block more than a few times.*

Q: Why do so many 40-year-olds brag about how well they did in school?

A: *Revisionist history.*

Q: What's the difference between a teenager and a 40-year-old?

A: *One has an immediate smart-aleck reply, and the other thinks of a smart-aleck reply three hours later.*

Q: What's the difference between a 21-year-old and a 40-year-old?

A: *One's idea of a good time is partying until dawn, and the other's is not getting up to go to the bathroom until dawn.*

Q: Why do 40-year-olds claim, "Forty isn't as old as it used to be"?

A: *Denial always comes before acceptance.*

Q: What does a 40-year-old woman never forget?

A: *The last time she was carded.*

Q: What do you call a 40-year-old hopping on one leg and singing the national anthem?

A: *Old. It doesn't matter what he's doing—he's old.*

Q: What's the difference between a teenager and a 40-year-old?

A: *One gets up late, and one gets up slow.*

Q: Why does a book about turning 40 have to be brief?

A: *Because at this stage in life, one's attention...span...is...* Hey! Pay attention! *Because at this stage in life, one's attention span is very short!*

Q: Why do 40-year-olds get agitated when they hear the adage "You can't teach an old dog new tricks"?

A: *The last thing they want is to learn something new.*

Q: Why are 40-year-olds good parents for young children?

A: *They don't have the energy to sweat the small stuff.*

Q: What's the difference between aging and maturing?

A: *A fine wine matures. A whining 40-year-old just ages.*

Chapter 5

What's a Sure Sign You're 40?

Q: What's a sure sign you're 40?

A: *You* almost *boycotted the new Star Wars movies.*

Q: What's a sure sign you're 40?

A: *You now think you were dumb to have whined about turning 30.*

Q: What's a sure sign you're 40?

A: *You remember when cell phones cost hundreds of dollars and were the size—and weight—of bricks.*

Q: What's a sure sign you're 40?

A: *Like, you were once fluent in "Valley."*

Q: What's a sure sign you're 40?

A: *You're old enough to know you should look for the fine print in a contract, but too old to read it without bifocals.*

Q: What's a sure sign you're 40?

A: *Someone gave you this book.*

Q: What's a sure sign you're 40?

A: *You can't make out a single word of today's most popular songs.*

Q: What's a sure sign you're 40?

A: *When people tease you about your age, you make some of these comebacks: "Forty is only a number," "You're only as old as you feel," and "Bite me."*

Q: What's a sure sign you're 40?

A: *A coworker once told you, "You remind me of my dad."*

Q: What's a sure sign you're 40?

A: *You remember when Tom Hanks was on* Bosom Buddies *and Sarah Jessica Parker was on* Square Pegs.

Q: What's a sure sign you're 40?

A: *You've wandered a parking lot, frantically pushing the remote key, hoping your lost car will tell you where it is.*

Q: What's a sure sign you're 40?

A: *Your first camera used a flashcube.*

Q: What's a sure sign you're 40?

A: *You're still in love with Daisy Duke—the original, that is.*

Q: What's a sure sign you're 40?

A: *You no longer even try to fake it when you enter a room and can't for the life of you remember why.*

Q: What's a sure sign you're 40?

A: *Your kid recently pointed out you were driving with the blinker on.*

Chapter 6

On Your Birthday

Q: What's the surest way of looking young at your 40th birthday party?

A: *Don't invite anyone under 70.*

Q: How does a 40-year-old make sure she has a really great time at her birthday party?

A: *Before heading out, she drops a little antacid.*

Q: Did anyone ever look forward to turning 40?

A: *Yes. Back when the average life span was 35 years.*

Q: What's the best part of turning 40?

A: *It's not 50.*

Q: Does anyone besides 40-year-olds think birthday teasing should stop?

A: *Yes. 39-year-olds.*

Q: What's the only way to make 39-year-olds look forward to their next birthday?

A: *Change the legal retirement age to 40.*

Q: What does a 40-year-old really want on his birthday?

A: *A nap.*

Q: What's a gift that a 40-year-old can really use?

A: *A fake ID that lets her get senior discounts.*

Q: Why is it great to have your kids at your 40th birthday party?

A: *They won't tease you mercilessly; to them, you've always been old.*

Q: Why do coworkers insist on decorating with black balloons and crepe paper for your 40th birthday?

A: *They know how funny you thought it was when you did it for older staff members.*

Q: What's the key to a happy 40th birthday?

A: *Profusely thank family and friends for their gag gifts and then plot to save those items for that 38-year-old who won't stop laughing.*

Q: What's worse than hearing someone exclaim, "You're 40 today!"?

A: *Hearing, "You're only 40 today?*
Someone said you were turning 50!"

Q: So what's great about turning 40?

A: *It'll be ten full years before you feel this bad about another birthday.*

Q: What's good about turning 40?

A: *You made it to 40!*

Q: Why do people call this birthday the "Big Four-Oh"?

A: *It would be a little too discouraging if they called it the "Big Four-Uh-Oh."*

Q: What theme does a 40-year-old want for his party?

A: *"Happy 39th Birthday."*

Chapter 7
Middle Age

Q: How do you know 40 is old?

A: *30 seems young.*

Q: What ancient and time-honored concept do 40-year-olds suddenly embrace?

A: *Respect for elders.*

Q: What's a sure sign you're 40?

A: *You're convinced more people have started mumbling.*

Q: How do you make a 40-year-old cry?

A: *Explain how, technically, she's entering her fifth decade.*

Q: According to a 40-year-old, when does middle age begin?

A: *When he's exactly half the age of the oldest person listed in the* Guinness Book of World Records.

Q: What's a sure sign you've hit middle age?

A: *The clothes in the back of your closet are in style again.*

Q: What's the difference between a midlife crisis and temporary insanity?

A: *Temporary insanity can be used as a legal defense.*

Q: How do you know 40 is old?

A: *You no longer even notice when someone calls you "sir" or "ma'am."*

Q: What's a 40-year-old's ultimate defense?

A: *"But I don't feel 40."*

Q: How can a 40-year-old really make a 25-year-old laugh?

A: *By claiming, "40 is the new 25."*

Q: Why do 40-year-olds stick together?

A: *Everyone else tells them they're too old or too young to know anything.*

Q: Are there any ways to be considered young at age 40?

A: *Yes. Run for U.S. president or die.*

Q: What's great about turning 40?

A: *There's less likelihood of identity theft. Even crooks don't want to be your age.*

Q: Does everyone consider 40 old?

A: *No, only the majority of people on the planet, who happen to be younger than that.*

Q: But doesn't life begin at 40?

A: *That quote has been taken out of context. The complete line is, "The end of life begins at 40."*

Also from Meadowbrook Press

What You Don't Know about Turning 50...
This funny birthday quiz contains outrageous answers to 101 commonly asked questions about turning 50. Written by P. D. Witte and illustrated by Steve Mark, this book contains everything you always wanted to know about the big five-o.

What You Don't Know about Turning 60...
This funny birthday quiz contains outrageous answers to 101 commonly asked questions about turning 60. Written by P. D. Witte and illustrated by Steve Mark, this book contains everything you always wanted to know about the big six-o.

What You Don't Know about Retirement
Q: How can I make sure my friends and family stay in touch?
A: *Move to a vacation spot and live in a place with a pool.*
Q: Why is it dangerous for retirees to miss condo-owners association meetings?
A: *They might be elected president.*
Makes a great gift and provides a funny quiz to make any retirement party more fun.

www.meadowbrookpress.com

Meadowbrook Press • 6110 Blue Circle Drive, Suite 237 • Minnetonka, MN • 55343